Copyright © 2024: Victoria McGlone, Three Cliffs Inc.

All rights reserved.

No part of this publication may be reproduced, distributed, or transmitted in any form or by any means, including photocopying, recording, or other electronic or mechanical methods, without the prior written permission of the publisher, except as permitted by U.S. and Canadian copyright law. For permission requests, contact Victoria McGlone at Three Cliffs Inc.

The story, all names, characters, and incidents portrayed in this production are fictitious. No identification with actual persons (living or deceased), places, buildings, and products is intended or should be inferred.

Book Cover and Illustrations Copyright: Aanchal Lodhi
ISBN: 978-1-7382946-0-2

www.thegoodcancer.ca

The Good Cancer

By: Victoria McGlone

Illustrations: Aanchal Lodhi

The Good Cancer is dedicated to
Charlie and Lola.

Two courageous young children who
witnessed their mother battle breast cancer
at the young ages of just 8 and 6.
Charlie and Lola – your strength carried me
through my darkest days. You are the reason
and you are my heart.

– With love and gratitude forever,
Mum.

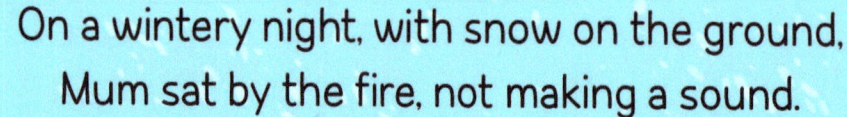

On a wintery night, with snow on the ground,
Mum sat by the fire, not making a sound.

There was sledding, snowballs, hot chocolate and games,
and gooey marshmallows held over the flames.
Daddy was laughing and squealing and jesting,
while Mummy was wrapped in a blanket, resting.

"Is Mum tired again?" asked Grace, politely,
as William raced by her, loud and unsightly.
"Yes, she is," said Dad. He had love in his eyes.
"Mum is going to need some help from you guys."

With sleds packed away and the fire burned out,
Grace shook Mum awake with a bit of a shout.

"Hey Mum, are you sleeping? You look a bit sick."
She asked, concerned, her voice sounding thick.

The time had come for their parents to explain,
that Mum's health was changing all over again.

She'd been feeling weak and very worn out,
which left the kids asking what it was about.

"The reason I'm tired and sleeping a lot,
is because my energy levels are shot.
It's not a headache, a burn or a bruise,
it's a little more serious than what we would choose."

"Mummy's been sick — it's called cancer," Dad said.
"We'll face it with courage, so don't hang your head.
There are many types of cancer, you see.
And Mum has the good kind, thankfully."

William was shocked. Grace felt scared.
For this conversation they were unprepared.
To learn Mummy was sick felt very confusing,
she was not someone they could imagine losing.

"Are you going to die?" asked William through tears.
"Are you going to be sick for years and years?"
He'd heard stories at school about others who'd passed,
he was looking for answers and wanted them fast.

"She won't pass away, I promise you so,
though the journey is tough, together we'll grow.
This challenge she faces, we'll conquer as one,
with love and support, until it is done."

"The medicine for Mummy is very strong. It will rid her of cancer and it won't take long.

There are some side effects you should know, to prepare yourselves for how things will go."

"First things first, we should talk about hair.
Soon she will lose hers, and her head will look bare.
She will likely feel tired and she'll sleep a lot.
That's normal to fight the Good Cancer she's got."

"One of the ways we can all help Mum best, is to give her the time and the space to rest.

She'll need lots of kisses and cuddles and hugs,
so she'll always remember how much she's loved."

"I can't wait to see you without any hair!"
Squealed Grace, as she grabbed her old teddy bear.

"You'll look like Kingsley, all fluffy and burly.
Your hair may even grow back very curly!"

"Can we buy you some wigs, a scarf or a hat?"
William thought Mummy would appreciate that.

"Great idea William!" Mummy smiled with glee,
imagining what her new style might be.

With night drawing in and the moon shining strong, William and Grace knew the road would be long.

Grace yawned wide. William felt sleepy.
Daddy was strong. Mummy looked weepy.

"I love you both," said Mum, with tears in her eyes.
"Our next few months will have lows and some highs.
We trust our doctors. They are skilled, kind and smart.
They know I'll fight cancer with all my heart."

"The Good Cancer is strong, but we are strong too.
We'll make sure Mummy stays here for both of you.
Right now, we must focus on sleeping and rest,
of all types of cancer, we know Mum has the best."

The moon was still bright as they turned the lights out,
now William and Grace knew, without a doubt:

That Mummy was sick, but it wouldn't last forever.
The Good Cancer, you see, will always get better.

MEET THE FAMiLY

2023

About the Author

Victoria McGlone is a wife, mother and breast cancer survivor from Ottawa, Canada. Victoria was diagnosed with early-stage breast cancer at the age of 38, and during treatment, made it her mission to help other families with young children navigate their own complex and emotional journeys.

About the Illustrator

Aanchal Lodhi is an Indian picture book illustrator and surface pattern designer. Her work consists of bright, whimsical, and oh-so-cute illustrations!

www.ingramcontent.com/pod-product-compliance
Lightning Source LLC
Chambersburg PA
CBHW041712160426
43209CB00018B/1816